THE
Power *of* Our Words

F O R

Middle School

Teacher Language That Helps
Students Learn

Responsive Classroom®
MIDDLE SCHOOL

All net proceeds from the sale of this book support the work of Center for Responsive Schools, Inc., a not-for-profit educational organization and the developer of the *Responsive Classroom*® approach to teaching.

The stories in this book are all based on real events. However, to respect students' privacy, names and many identifying characteristics of students and situations have been changed.

ISBN: 978-1-892989-86-4
Library of Congress Control Number: 2016930142

Photographs by Jeff Woodward

Center for Responsive Schools wishes to thank the many people whose hard work and dedication to students and educators have made this book possible. Special thanks go to middle grades educators Kimberly Eiseman and Sue French for their careful reading of and feedback on the manuscript.

Center for Responsive Schools, Inc.
85 Avenue A, P.O. Box 718
Turners Falls, MA 01376-0718

800-360-6332
www.responsiveclassroom.org

Second printing 2016

TABLE OF CONTENTS

1

Getting the Most From Teacher Language

Using Our Words to Make a Difference

"Good morning astronomers. We're about to begin our unit on the use of robotics in space exploration. I'm looking forward to helping you discover some answers to what was once the unknown."

"I see everyone with materials on their desks, ready to begin."

"Before we use these supplies again, who can remind us what our safety rules are?"

What Is Teacher Language?

Language is more than the simple expression of thoughts, feelings, and experiences. According to psychologist Lev Vygotsky, language actually molds our sense of who we are, helps us understand how we work and play, and influences the nature of our relationships—producing "fundamentally new forms of behavior" (Vygotsky, 1978, p. 24).

The term "teacher language" refers specifically to the professional use of words, phrases, and tone that enables students to more fully engage in their learning; to become contributing members of a positive learning community; and to develop the academic, social, and emotional learning skills needed for success in and out of school. Teacher language rests on a deep, abiding faith in the goodness of adolescents, in their desire and ability to learn, and in our ability to teach and bring out the best in all students.

The chapters that follow explore five types of teacher language:

➤ **Chapter 2: Envisioning language**—helps students create positive mental images of themselves achieving and behaving in ways that connect to and then go beyond their current reality.

> **EXAMPLE:** "We've been talking about respect. What will it look and sound like in this class to treat each other with respect?"

➤ **Chapter 3: Reinforcing language**—names exactly what students are doing well so they can build on their successes and develop a sense of themselves as competent learners, which helps students move to higher levels of competence.

> **EXAMPLE:** "You added concrete evidence to your essay and that makes for a stronger argument."

➤ **Chapter 4: Reminding language**—prompts students to independently recall the specific things they need to do to meet academic and behavioral expectations.

> **EXAMPLE:** "What are some things you can do so that all group members' ideas are considered fairly?"

➤ **Chapter 5: Redirecting language**—directs students back to productive learning when their behavior has gone off task, while helping the rest of the class stay focused on their learning.

> **EXAMPLE:** "Hands down until the speaker has finished."

➤ **Chapter 6: Open-ended questions**—have no right or wrong answer, thus stretching students' curiosity, reasoning ability, creativity, and independence so that they learn more broadly and deeply.

> **EXAMPLE:** "What are you most proud of about your work, and why?"

Why Our Words Matter to Students

Our words hold more power than we may realize. Because language permeates nearly every interaction between teachers and students, it shapes how students think about themselves and school, how they act, and how they learn. Intentionally weaving positive language into our teaching enables us to promote students' growth and learning in three key areas:

➤ Academic skills and content knowledge

➤ Social and emotional learning skills

➤ Collaboration and community

Across all of these areas, language allows us to articulate a vision, convey faith that students can attain that vision, give feedback that names students' strengths, and offer guidance that expands their skills, knowledge, and confidence. Specifically, teacher language:

➤ **Helps students build positive identities**—What we say to students can deeply affect their sense of who they are and who they might become: scientists, writers, musicians, entrepreneurs, leaders. When we focus on the positives in students, we can inspire them to develop the skills they need to achieve their goals, turning hopes into realities.

➤ **Expands students' thinking**—Our words can help students understand how they think and work, giving them insight into what they are capable of and how they can articulate and achieve academic, social, and behavioral goals.

➤ **Builds trust between us and our students**—When we invite students' questions, ideas, and feedback and maintain a respectful dialogue, we gain more insight into their lives and forge more trusting relationships. Greater trust, in turn, leads to more prosocial and positive academic behaviors, especially self-motivation and autonomy.

➤ **Promotes positive peer-to-peer relationships**—Our words and tone can create an atmosphere of respectful interactions among all students. By influencing them to become self-motivated learners and to value their peers, we can promote deeper and more engaged learning while also building a sense of belonging and community.

➤ **Influences students to use language skillfully themselves**—When we model the positive use of language, our students pick up on that and start to use positive language themselves. The result is that the classroom becomes a richer place of collaboration, with students actively helping each other learn and grow.

Clearly, positive language is a powerful teaching tool. By harnessing this power, we can open the doors of possibility and hope for young adolescents and help them develop into capable and confident lifelong learners.

How to Use Teacher Language Effectively

Be direct and genuine

When we say what we mean directly and respectfully, students understand our expectations and learn that they can trust us. We need to:

➤ **Speak in a matter-of-fact tone and match body language to words.** Letting anger or frustration creep into our voices can cause students to feel confused, humiliated, or resentful. Students are quick to pick up on our gestures, postures, and expressions. If these don't sync up to our words, students will start to distrust us.

➤ **Avoid manipulation, sarcasm, and labels.** Think of the impact on students of "Jena, you could learn a thing or two from Mia" compared with "Jena, it looks like you're stuck. What do you think might help you work through this?" Also, because students tend to be confused or upset by adult sarcasm, using appropriate humor or a straightforward approach can work better. And naming characteristics or making general statements ("that's lazy") can be like sticking a label on someone—and labels are hard to remove.

➤ **Use statements, not questions, when giving directions or redirections.** Unless we are really giving students a choice, it's best to simply be direct with them. Instead of "Would you take your seat, Sara?" we simply say, "Sara, take your seat."

➤ **Follow through.** When we direct students to do something, we need to make sure they do it. Consistency in following through communicates to students that they need to take our words seriously.

> **EXAMPLE:** If we expect students to use quiet voices in small groups and voices start to rise, we need to hold them to this expectation, rather than ignoring the louder voices and hoping students will quiet down: "One of our small group rules is 'Use quiet voices.' Lower your voices."

Convey faith in students' abilities and intentions

When we take time to notice and comment on the things students do well, we let them know we have confidence in them and provide concrete evidence why they should believe in themselves, too. When students believe in themselves, they're more likely to work hard at learning and enjoy the process. It's important to:

➤ **Take time to notice the positives.** The positive behaviors we notice and point out to students are most likely the behaviors they'll repeat.

> **EXAMPLE:** "You included valid reasons and supporting evidence in your essays."

➤ **Avoid condescending talk.** Middle schoolers want and deserve to be spoken to as young adults. Consider the impact on students of "Thank you, hon" compared with a sincere "Thank you, John" or a simple "Thank you."

➤ **Be aware of language that might suggest bias or stereotypes.** Are we asking boys to do physically demanding tasks like moving furniture while asking girls to do artistic tasks like making posters? For personal and professional growth, we continually want to ask ourselves: "Could my words be limiting how I view students and how students perceive themselves?"

Focus on behavior

When we connect abstract terms ("Be respectful") with concrete behaviors ("Remember to provide positive feedback"), we enable students to learn at their best. And when we have taught and modeled desired behaviors, we can then prompt students to name concrete, positive behaviors themselves.

➤ **Describe behavior, not character.** By issuing positive challenges, we can better focus students on what they're capable of doing.

> **EXAMPLE:** Think about the effect on students' motivation if we say, "I don't think you're even trying!" compared with "Let's see if you can think of a way to get excited about this assignment. What would help you do that?"

➤ **Be nonjudgmental.** Sometimes our words contain hidden judgments.

> **EXAMPLE:** "If you really tried, you could do this" signals to students that we believe they don't care enough to make an effort. We can be more helpful to students if we describe what we're noticing in nonjudgmental terms and give students the opportunity to work with us on finding a solution: "I noticed that you didn't finish problem five. What would help you complete it?"

Keep it precise, simple, brief, and positive

Students understand more when we speak less. Long explanations, however reasoned and well-intentioned, are usually counterproductive because students often start to think about other things before we finish talking. We may also be tempted to warn students what might happen if they don't heed reminders and redirections, but such warnings are generally not effective and too often come across like threats. When speaking to young adults, it's best to:

➤ **Use fewer words.** For most students, the longer we talk, the less they hear. Compare "It's really important that you follow the safety procedures we talked about yesterday. First . . . Second . . . Third . . . And one last thing, don't forget any of these steps because . . ." with "Who can tell us the three safety steps we talked about yesterday?"

Knowing When to Be Silent

Silence allows for all students' voices to be heard. It gives them time to think, plan what to say, and sometimes even gather the courage to speak at all. Our silence:

1. **Provides valuable wait time.** Students need time to process what we've said and compose thoughtful responses. By simply pausing three to five seconds before calling on students, we can raise the quality of classroom conversations.

2. **Helps us really listen to students.** Not only do we model respectful inter-action in a community of learners, but our listening actually helps students learn. That's because speaking is a way for them to gain knowledge and de-velop understanding.

3. **Keeps us from repeating directions.** Students develop greater autonomy when given chances to remember directions for themselves and experi-ence the consequences of either remembering or forgetting.

4. **Reduces the use of voice-overs.** When we repeat a student's answer—for example, if a student says, "The year was 1776" and we say, "Yes, 1776"—we send the unintional message that a student's words matter only if an adult repeats them. Letting students' voices stand on their own establishes that it's important for everyone to listen to each other.

Silence is essential to the development of a strong classroom community and a calm, orderly environment that's conducive to learning.

> **Get right to the point.** It's best to leave out the preambles so students can focus on exactly what's expected.

> **EXAMPLE:** Compare "Juan, we're supposed to be working in our groups now, so you should be working with Maya's group" with "Juan, join Maya's group."

> **Leave out threats or warnings.** These undermine students' self-confidence and diminish their willing-ness to take responsibility for their actions. One way to support students is by focusing on finding a solution when they don't meet expectations.

> **EXAMPLE:** "Nick, your homework is missing for the second time this week. Let's check in and make a plan so this doesn't happen again."

The Process of Changing Our Language

Changing language habits takes time and practice. Be patient with yourself; the more you use positive teacher language, the more proficient you'll become.

Stages of Changing Teacher Language

> **Knowing why teacher language matters**—We begin to notice aspects of our language that we want to keep and those we want to change, such as general praise ("Great work"), sarcasm ("Thanks so much for interrupting me"), and unconscious biases (such as using different language for boys and girls).

> **Deciding to make a change**—In this stage, we start to catch ourselves when we use language we want to change. We start to do simple, silent rehearsals of more constructive language to try next time.

> **Increasing the use of productive language**—As we continue to learn and practice we become more aware of our words, quickly catching counter-

productive language ("Class is half over and you haven't done any work!") and replacing it with more skillful, language that better meets our goals ("Oops! Let me rephrase that. You've completed five of the problems. What strategies can you use to help you finish the rest before class ends?"). We also start to notice how the changes we're making are benefitting students.

➤ **Thinking in new language patterns**—The more we use positive teacher language, the more natural it becomes. Eventually, it will flow more easily and truly express our positive approach to teaching.

Tips for Changing Language

1. **Record yourself in the classroom** for short periods each day. Play back the recording and listen to your words and tone.

2. **Set reasonable goals.** Focus on one aspect at a time, such as using more reinforcing language (Chapter 3). Ask a colleague, teachers on your team, or the whole staff to join you.

3. **Practice in the moment** when you say a word or phrase you'd rather not say. Try to quickly replace the word or phrase with something more constructive.

4. **Use signals to get students' attention** instead of using words. This gives you some time to come up with constructive words to use.

5. **Take a breath** (or three) and think before you speak.

Changing Words, Changing Lives

The language we use with students every day influences how they see themselves, their teachers, their classmates, and their experiences with learning. By paying attention to the power of our language—and using it to open the doors of possibility for students—we help them become self-confident, engaged learners. Our words can make such a positive difference in our teaching and students' learning.

WORK CITED

Vygotsky, L. (1978). *Mind in Society*. Cambridge, MA: Harvard University Press.

2

Envisioning Language

Giving Students a Vision of What's Possible

"I hope that by the end of this unit everyone will feel confident about solving one-variable equations."

"What would it look, sound, and feel like if people were being respectful to one another during our class discussions?"

"You've all been asking very thoughtful questions about climate change, just like scientists do. That's really going to help you plan your research experiments."

What Is Envisioning Language?

Statements and questions that help students create positive mental images of themselves are at the heart of envisioning language. This language works by helping students see themselves achieving and behaving in ways that connect to, but go beyond, what they already know and can do.

The Power of Envisioning Language

Envisioning language reaches beyond textbooks, assignments, and grades by speaking to students' deepest human needs and dreams. Just like adults, students want to become knowledgeable, competent, and autonomous learners and citizens. They want to feel engaged and passionate about something that matters to them and to their community and to feel that they can make a difference in the world.

Envisioning statements can tap into students' lives *beyond* school, thus helping them connect more powerfully *to* school. These statements give students an exciting picture of what's possible and enable them to see that they can solve academic and social problems and achieve something bigger and brighter than their current reality. Envisioning language:

➤ **Inspires effort and persistence**—Envisioning language inspires students to work hard by helping them see the possible positive outcomes of their efforts. This language can be especially inspirational for students during the rapid physical and cognitive changes and growing social pressures of the middle school years—a time when many struggle with self-motivation. When students' motivation wanes, envisioning language can encourage them to persist in putting forth their best efforts by reminding them of both their achievements and their goals.

> **EXAMPLE:** "Many of you have shared your interest in engineering. As you worked on this unit, you made some connections to engineering. You'll be able to study those in more depth when we start our next unit."

➤ **Sets a positive tone for learning**—We can use envisioning language to frame new learning in ways that help students see what they already do well and where those capabilities can take them. With this sense of themselves as competent learners, students are more likely to succeed in new undertakings. It's equally effective whether the undertaking is broad (being successful with a new curriculum unit) or narrow (having a productive math period).

> **EXAMPLE:** To students about to move up a level in algebraic problem-solving, a teacher might say, "We're about to start working on solving two-variable equations. Given how well you've done with one-variable equations, I believe you have the strategies you'll need to meet this new challenge successfully."

Envisioning language can also be used to set a positive tone when students are working on the social-emotional skills needed for school success.

> **EXAMPLE:** "Successful teams don't always agree on a solution, but they do value everyone's opinions. You've made great progress showing that kind of respect to your partners. Now what are some things you can do to transfer those skills to your groups?"

➤ **Builds a sense of belonging and community**—Because middle schoolers are often quite sensitive to how they're perceived by others, it's important for them to feel that they're welcomed and important members of their learning community. Only then will they feel comfortable taking the risks and engaging in the cooperative give-and-take essential to learning. We can foster students' sense of belonging by using envisioning language that encourages the whole class to value and practice cooperation, respect, and empathy.

> **EXAMPLE:** "Great discoveries usually come from teams, rather than one person working alone. That's because everyone contributes a different perspective and different skills. So that's your challenge this year: working together, valuing everyone's input, and keeping the focus on finding solutions to the issues we'll be studying."

Through envisioning language, we can have a positive impact on our students' lives, inspiring them and giving them hope.

Envisioning Language Sentence Starters

➤ I hope that _____.

➤ Imagine that you _____.

➤ What needs to happen so everyone can _____?

➤ You're going to be [name the activity]. How will you do that successfully?

➤ Think about what you would be doing if you were a professional _____.

➤ What will make your _____ successful?

How to Use Envisioning Language Effectively

Connect with students' interests and aspirations

The more we know our students, the more we can use that knowledge to help students connect the work of school to those things they value and care most deeply about—forming strong friendships; contributing to their family, community, and the wider world; and gaining knowledge and skills in academic areas that interest them.

SITUATION	ENVISIONING LANGUAGE
One class loves sports and they're about to work in small groups.	"You know how sports teams play much better when all the players work together? Your groups will get the best results if you also work like a team."

SITUATION	ENVISIONING LANGUAGE
Another class is especially interested in social justice issues but they often talk over one another during discussions.	"I know that fairness matters to you. So, what can we do to make sure that everyone's voices get heard as we discuss the article we just read?"

NOTES / REFLECTIONS

Name positive identities for students

Addressing students as "writers," "creative thinkers," or "problem-solvers" can motivate them to live up to the positives represented by such terms. Keep in mind that students will want to live up to the identities you name only if they sense that you truly believe they can. So be sure that your envisioning language names skills, capabilities, and behaviors you're convinced are within students' reach.

SITUATION	ENVISIONING LANGUAGE
A science class is meeting for the first time at the beginning of a new semester.	"Welcome, engineers. This semester, we'll be building on the curiosity and inventiveness you demonstrated last semester as we use technology to solve some real-world problems."

SITUATION	ENVISIONING LANGUAGE
Students are about to start working in pairs on an experiment.	"OK, scientists, your research proposals show that you really understand how to formulate a testable hypothesis. Now find your partner and decide what resources you'll need to set up your experiments."

NOTES / REFLECTIONS

Use concrete images and terms students relate to

Abstract terms—*show respect, be responsible, get motivated*—won't automatically create a clear vision in students' minds, especially if we overuse these terms. Instead, aim for specific, precise language that draws on words students themselves actually use. You can do this by asking students why they think something is important and then using their own words to frame an envisioning statement.

SITUATION	ENVISIONING LANGUAGE
Students are using putdowns with each other—and your telling them to "be respectful" isn't working. After listening to what respect means to them, you use their words to name a new vision.	"You're saying that 'respect' means everyone feels comfortable being who they are. Let's brainstorm: What things can we all say and do to make sure everyone has that same sense of comfort?"

SITUATION	ENVISIONING LANGUAGE
Students are starting a new unit of study.	"We're about to learn about infectious diseases and the germs that cause them. Why can learning about something that might seem disgusting or depressing be valuable to us in our lives?"

NOTES / REFLECTIONS

Prompt students to fill in the details

Visions become reality only when our actions bring them to life. For example, students can become knowledgeable about their research topics only if they make the effort to find reliable sources, synthesize ideas, write, and revise. We could simply tell students what steps to take to achieve this goal, but they'll be much more motivated if we encourage them to come up with some specifics for themselves. Inviting students to do this thinking also shows our faith in their capabilities and support for their growing independence.

SITUATION	ENVISIONING LANGUAGE
You are going to assign students a short research project and you know that most students have *limited experience* with research.	"What should you think about as you plan your research? What resources would you need for finding the most reliable information? Who here in this class or elsewhere in school might have helpful ideas?"

SITUATION	ENVISIONING LANGUAGE
You are going to assign students a short research project and you know that most students have *successfully* done these.	"Before you set out on your research, think about what you'll need to do to bring new perspectives to your topic."

NOTES / REFLECTIONS

When You Might Use Envisioning Language

In this situation	Try
Before students work on their own	"You've seen how focusing on your work pays off. What do you need to do to keep your focus on this assignment?" ✳ *Names current skills students can build on; invites students to fill in the details.*
Before transitions	"Like professional scientists, you've taken great care in using the equipment today. I know you'll be just as careful when you put it away so that you'll have it ready to finish your experiments tomorrow." ✳ *Names a positive identity; expresses confidence in students' capabilities.*
Before whole-group discussions/ activities	"Mathematical thinkers are always looking for ways to solve problems with fewer steps. What's one way this kind of thinking could help you in this math challenge? What about in a hobby or activity you do outside school?" ✳ *Names a positive identity; invites students to fill in the details; connects to things that matter in their personal lives.* ――――― "You've read many different authors so far this semester and analyzed their work. What would you have to do to capture a favorite author's style in your own writing?" ✳ *Recognizes students' accomplishments; invites them to fill in the details.*

In this situation	Try
Before small-group learning	"All right, analysts, this next group project will give you an opportunity to share ideas and expand your thinking skills." ✳ *Names a positive identity; names current skills that the teacher believes students can build on.*
At the start of a new unit	"Food makes a huge difference in the fitness of our brains as well as our bodies. I bet you'll come up with some important connections between what you eat each day and how you think and feel." ✳ *Connects to students' needs and aspirations; expresses confidence in students' capabilities.*
Before students begin a challenging task	"Public speaking does require us to use some skills we don't practice every day, so let's brainstorm: What do you think skilled speakers do to keep themselves calm and focused?" ✳ *Suggests a positive identity; invites students to fill in the details.*
During a lesson	"As you continue to build your problem-solving skills, see how many different strategies you can come up with as a group." ✳ *Sets a positive tone; recognizes what students have already accomplished and can build on.*
In one-on-one conversations with you	"I've seen you be a supportive partner in the past. What can you do to offer Tonya that same kind of support?" ✳ *Names a positive identity; invites the student to fill in the details.*

Envisioning Language (continued)

In this situation	Try
When teaching behavior	"Our class rule says we'll be considerate to one another when we work in small groups. Think about what your groups would look and sound like if everyone is being considerate and supportive." ✳ *Connects to values expressed in a rule that matters to students; invites students to fill in the details.*
When teaching routines	"You've all been careful and thorough in following our routines for cleaning and putting away the supplies we've used so far. I believe you'll be just as careful and thorough with the new supplies we'll be using for this next project." ✳ *Recognizes students' accomplishments; expresses confidence in their ability; names a positive identity.*

Tips for Strengthening Envisioning Language

As you (and students) become comfortable with envisioning language, try these techniques for making your statements and questions even more engaging and compelling.

Steer clear of overly emphasizing grades

Although grades are important, putting too much emphasis on them can backfire, with some students becoming very competitive and others getting discouraged. Instead, we can use envisioning language to inspire students to find their own internal motivation, which then leads to better work habits, greater effort, and more success.

> **EXAMPLE:** Instead of saying "You're such a good student; you can get all A's," try "You work hard and enjoy digging deeper into your studies; what are your goals for this semester? What's something you want to get better at doing?"

Using Other Modes of Expression

If students struggle to verbalize their goals, interests, or aspirations, suggest they present them in another way, perhaps by drawing or composing a song. The method matters less than your support as they sort out what truly matters to them.

Incorporate metaphors

Metaphors—figures of speech that explain one idea in terms of another—can add power and clarity to envisioning language. Using metaphors can prompt students to think more broadly and imaginatively and inspire them to take the positive actions expressed by the metaphor. Look for metaphors that will have meaning for your students; you can draw them from art, literature, sports, history, the current curriculum, classroom experiences, and students' daily lives.

> **EXAMPLE:** To a student who's struggling to persist when work becomes more challenging, we might say, "Remember the video that showed surfers riding on those giant, rough waves? There's always going to be some rough water now and then. What could you do to stay on your board, no matter what the waves are doing?"

Avoid comparing positive identities to negative ones

When a negative lable is paired with a positive one ("Good writers are not careless writers"), the negative label often carries more weight or causes students to feel resentful. As a result, they may stop trying to reach for the positive vision.

> **EXAMPLE:** Instead of saying "I'm hoping to see people working hard and no one being lazy," try "What does making a quality effort look and feel like?"

Envisioning Language Practice Chart

Jot down ideas for envisioning language you might use with the scenarios given below or adapt language used in the examples on the previous pages. There is also space for you to write your own scenarios and envisioning language you might use with them.

SCENARIO	ENVISIONING LANGUAGE
Students are about to begin a new unit of study.	
Students are going to be working on a challenging assignment.	
Students are going to be working with a new partner or in a new small group.	
Your scenario:	
Your scenario:	

Envisioning Language Self-Reflection Chart

For a week, keep the following chart handy to track how often you use envisioning language (use check marks or tally marks). You can also rate yourself to see your growth. Don't worry about keeping an exact count—and stay positive—improving teacher language takes time. With each day you try it, you'll see the results it brings and start to feel more and more comfortable using it.

	Number of times I used envisioning language	Opportunities I missed when I could have used envisioning language	Rating my effective use of envisioning language 1 = emerging 3 = developing 5 = achieving
Monday			
Tuesday			
Wednesday			
Thursday			
Friday			
Totals			
Notes			

3

Reinforcing Language
Helping Students Move to Higher Levels

"I noticed speakers pointing out specific facts from the articles to support their ideas. What else did you notice speakers doing to communicate effectively?"

"You remembered to speak one at a time today. That really helped us hear everyone's ideas and kept the discussion going smoothly."

"You found several different solutions to today's geometry challenge. That persistence will help you solve our next set of problems."

What Is Reinforcing Language?

Reinforcing language is a way of using our words to identify and affirm students' specific, positive actions. This language spells out exactly which academic and social behaviors students are doing well so that they're motivated to continue building on those behaviors.

The Power of Reinforcing Language

Reinforcing language focuses on students' strengths. In its specificity, reinforcing language moves beyond general praise—"Nice job!" "I like that!"—and offers precise information about what students have done well. By using reinforcing language to recognize students' positive actions, such as using a skill successfully or helping a classmate, we're giving students specific, useful feedback.

At its heart, reinforcing language is about encouraging student self-reflection and growth by objectively recognizing their efforts and accomplishments. This encouragement and recognition is particularly important for adolescents, who are in the midst of forming their young adult identity and figuring out how to be responsible and productive members of society. While encouraging insightful self-reflection, reinforcing language also shows students our genuine appreciation and respect for them as individuals.

Reinforcing language promotes engaged learning by encouraging students to:

➤ **Stay focused on practice and effort**—Our feedback should point out students' effort and incremental achievement rather than grades or final products. This helps students concentrate on the process of learning, showing them that if they persist in working hard, they will make progress and produce work they can be proud of.

➤ **Form a positive vision of themselves**—Reinforcing feedback inspires students to see their true capabilities as learners. Consider this example: "The teamwork you each showed today led directly to the significant progress you made in your group project." This type of language enables students to view themselves as valuable individuals and contributing team members.

➤ **Focus on their strengths**—Reinforcing language helps students recognize their own "internal muscles" and learn how to use these assets to tackle new challenges. As a result, they start to develop an understanding that ability and success are less about "being smart" and much more about hard work, persistence, and a positive attitude.

➤ **Become more self-motivated**—Reinforcing language prompts students to reflect on their actions, think more deeply about the learning process, and name for themselves what they did well in reaching toward their goals. This reflection can motivate them to take more ownership of their schoolwork.

By giving students specific, positive feedback about their growth and effort, reinforcing language can transform how they view practice and persistence and increase their motivation. This powerful language encourages them to take the risks and put in the work necessary to learn something new, master a skill, and grow as young adults.

How to Use Reinforcing Language Effectively

Find positives to name in all students

One key to using reinforcing language effectively is to carefully observe students so we can highlight the positives we notice in their attitudes and efforts. Reinforcing language will not apply equally to all students at all times; yet, over time, it's important to see and encourage positive aspects of every student's behavior, whether they're taking small steps or making big leaps.

We also want to avoid singling out one or two students, which can lead to a competitive environment by elevating some students while discouraging others: If only a few students are named for doing things "right," then the others must be doing things "wrong."

SITUATION	REINFORCING LANGUAGE
Jackson struggles with correct word order when translating sentences from Spanish to English. Today he's gotten the right order in four out of seven sentences.	*(privately)* "Jackson, I noticed that you got exactly the right word order in several of your translations today. What strategies did you use to make that happen?"
Two students who tend not to get along are working well together on an assignment.	*(privately)* "Sam, Toni, you're using friendly, respectful words with each other. That's helping you make good progress on your assignment."

NOTES / REFLECTIONS

Emphasize description, not personal approval

Reinforcing language shifts the focus to students and what actions and behaviors are helping them succeed. Describing actions—rather than what we think or how we feel about students' efforts—helps strengthen their development as self-motivated, responsible learners.

SITUATION	REINFORCING LANGUAGE
A student who often has difficulty differentiating between fact and opinion writes an essay with concrete evidence that supports her argument.	*(privately)* "Felicity, you included lots of specific details in your paper. All your research really paid off."
SITUATION	REINFORCING LANGUAGE
Two students who usually don't take initiative use their own time to research the answer to a question that had stumped the whole class.	*(privately)* "Althea, Matt, choosing to take on this task all on your own showed great initiative. That kind of effort will help you in all your classes."

NOTES / REFLECTIONS

Name concrete and specific behaviors

We're more likely to promote growth if we give students precise information about what they're doing well instead of general praise ("I love it" or "Great job"). Identifying specific, positive actions helps students become more aware of what they know, their skills, and their progress.

When reinforcing individual students, it's best to do so in private so these students don't feel singled out (and so the rest of the class doesn't feel overlooked). When we want to reinforce the whole class because most students are putting forth positive efforts, we can do so publicly.

SITUATION	REINFORCING LANGUAGE
A student is making steady progress on his research paper.	*(privately)* "Sasha, I see that you took detailed notes on the articles. What have you decided to do next?"

SITUATION	REINFORCING LANGUAGE
The class is having an animated but respectful whole-group discussion.	"People were patient and waited for their turn before speaking. I also noticed people were thoughtfully adding on to what others said to help the discussion go deeper."

NOTES / REFLECTIONS

When Praise Is OK

There's still a time for general praise such as "Great game!" or "That's beautiful." When our purpose is not to guide behavior but to celebrate a success or show appreciation, then general praise can be appropriate. When we want to influence students' behavior, however, it's most effective to steer clear of such language and use specific, reinforcing language instead.

Point out student progress toward mastery

When students are engaged in learning content, they're often working toward mastering both academic and social skills. It's important to observe students and then use reinforcing language to point out their growth (and steer clear of focusing on where they came up short).

Over time, our positive observations give students a foundation to build upon as they move from proficiency to mastery.

SITUATION	REINFORCING LANGUAGE
Only a few students are sharing ideas during a class discussion.	"We heard several insightful ideas about why the main character is having such a moral dilemma. Let's hear some other points of view."

SITUATION	REINFORCING LANGUAGE
A student who has difficulty finishing in-class work within the allotted time has most of the problems completed before class ends.	(*privately*) "I noticed you worked hard to complete those five problems. What do you think helped you complete them?"

NOTES / REFLECTIONS

Use a question to extend students' thinking

Following positive feedback with an open-ended question (see Chapter 6) prompts reflection and encourages students to extend their thinking. Your question can help students become more aware of the behavior you named and how it's helpful to them, or it might encourage them to see what they can do to advance even further.

SITUATION	REINFORCING LANGUAGE
Two students brainstorm ways to illustrate the results of their science experiment.	(*privately*) "Tamika, Inez, I noticed you came up with lots of ideas for illustrating your results section. What enabled you two to collaborate so effectively?"

SITUATION	REINFORCING LANGUAGE
Jamal gives an effective presentation.	(*privately*) "Jamal, your classmates were really focused on you as you presented. What did you do that grabbed everyone's attention?"

NOTES / REFLECTIONS

Reinforcing Language Sentence Starters

➤ I noticed _____.

➤ I see that _____.

➤ You remembered to _____.

➤ You all helped to _____.

➤ You paid attention to _____.

➤ You followed our rule by _____.

➤ Did you notice _____?

➤ One of the reasons your group was successful today was _____.

➤ Because you _____, your work _____.

When You Might Use Reinforcing Language

In this situation	Instead of	Try
When students are working on their own	"Really good work. You're quite smart!" ✴ *Gives general praise and attributes the student's success to being smart, instead of to effort.*	"You worked hard to put in a lot of detail." ✴ *Names a specific, helpful behavior and attributes the student's success to effort.*
During small-group learning	"I liked your answers to my discussion questions." ✴ *Focuses on the teacher's personal approval.*	"You backed up your answers with evidence from our reading." ✴ *Focuses specifically on what students did well.*
During whole-group discussions/ activities	"You know, only Juan, Ella, and Sonya are paying attention. The rest of you are causing too many interruptions." ✴ *Names only a few students, which may embarrass them, and sends a negative message to other students, which may cause resentment and inhibit future participation.*	"I noticed some people turned their bodies toward the person speaking. That's one way to stay focused during a discussion. What are some other strategies you can use to stay focused?" ✴ *Names a specific, positive action that you observed and uses an open-ended question to invite positive reflection from the whole class.*

In this situation	Instead of	Try
In one-on-one conversations with you	"You're too smart to only have a C in this class." ✳ *Focuses on an abstract quality and emphasizes the final product at the expense of the learning process.*	"Your participation and homework completion have increased significantly during this unit of study. Do you remember your goals for this unit? Your effort and persistence are helping you achieve them." ✳ *Focuses on a specific, positive change the student is making and ties it to goals, which helps the student become even more self-motivated.*
During transitions	"Hurry up! You're wasting my time." ✳ *Focuses on what students are not doing well.*	"I see more and more students putting away their tablets and folders." ✳ *Focuses on the positive steps the teacher has observed.*

Tips for Strengthening Reinforcing Language

Reinforce individual students' actions privately, even if it means waiting to do so

Ideally we'd use reinforcing language in the moment, but sometimes we may need to wait until we can speak to the student privately.

EXAMPLE: Let's say that we noticed how Felix actively participated during a class discussion. If we acknowledge Felix publically, he may feel embarrassed or manipulated into serving as the class role model—and other students may feel overlooked or resentful (*I participated, but you didn't recognize me!*).

Our words would make a much more positive impact if we were to wait until we could approach Felix privately, such as during a transition, and say quietly, "You waited for a pause in the conversation to ask your question and that helped everyone stay on track."

Use a warm and professional tone

Sometimes when we try to show appreciation for students' efforts, we use language ("Thanks, hon" or "Good job, kiddos") that can feel childish or patronizing to them. Similarly, even if we intend to be funny, a statement such as "Wow, you were so attentive to today's speaker!" can be hurtful or embarrassing to students, especially with their heightened concern about peers' opinions of them.

Our positive communications with young adolescents can be more effective when we convey genuine appreciation for their efforts by using a warm tone and respectful words: "Some of you shared your thoughts today; many of you listened respectfully. What else did you do that helped us have such a thoughtful discussion?"

Name behaviors you actually notice, not ones you hope to see

Reinforcing language helps students learn and grow when we point out positive behaviors we see in them, even if these behaviors are not "perfect." Although it can be tempting to name a positive behavior we want students to demonstrate but haven't seen yet, this tactic can feel manipulative to them.

EXAMPLE: If we notice a lot of students speaking out of turn, saying "I see students waiting their turn to talk" in hopes of getting them to change course can be confusing and may even sound sarcastic.

In this kind of situation, we'd do better by using redirecting language (Chapter 5) to get them back on task: "Everyone stop. Discussion rules. Wait your turn to speak." Then, when we notice what students are actually doing well and point this out to them—"You debated this topic respectfully by actively listening and acknowledging each other's arguments even when you didn't agree"—they'll be more motivated to keep building on those behaviors.

Be selective in what you reinforce

Showering students with positive feedback by mentioning every little thing they do well lessens the power of our words. Also, we want to focus on reinforcing the behaviors that are truly essential to each student's individual growth.

EXAMPLE: If Vivian consistently gets right to work on the posted assignment, she doesn't need us to reinforce her efforts every time. In contrast, if Thomas usually procrastinates, he'll benefit from our reinforcing his efforts each time he gets to work right away.

Reinforcing Language Practice Chart

Jot down ideas for reinforcing language you might use with the scenarios given below or adapt language used in the examples on the previous pages. There is also space for you to write your own scenarios and reinforcing language you might use with them.

SCENARIO	REINFORCING LANGUAGE
After struggling to get started, a student makes steady progress on her presentation.	
As you observe small-group discussions, you notice that many groups are referring to the article they just read for evidence to support their ideas.	
While students work on individual projects, a student offers to help a classmate get started because he came in late.	
Your scenario:	
Your scenario:	

Reinforcing Language Self-Reflection Chart

For a week, keep the following chart handy to track how often you use reinforcing language (use check marks or tally marks). You can also rate yourself to see your growth. Don't worry about keeping an exact count, and stay positive—improving teacher language takes time. With each day you try it, you'll see the results it brings and begin to feel more and more comfortable using it.

	Number of times I used reinforcing language	Opportunities I missed when I could have used reinforcing language	Rating my effective use of reinforcing language 1 = emerging 3 = developing 5 = achieving
Monday			
Tuesday			
Wednesday			
Thursday			
Friday			
Totals			
Notes			

4

Reminding Language
Guiding Students to Meet Expectations

"Think about the steps you'll need to complete the assignment on your own."

"Now that you've pre-viewed this article, take a minute to remember some strategies you can use to identify its key points."

"What's one way you can follow our discussion rules when you meet with your group today?"

What Is Reminding Language?

Reminding language consists of brief statements or questions that help students take responsibility for remembering and meeting expectations. As adults, we use sticky notes, electronic alerts, and other reminders to help us stay organized and on task in our personal and work lives. Similarly, teachers' reminders can help students successfully navigate the "must do's" of their busy school lives.

The Power of Reminding Language

There's one major difference between everyday reminders and the reminding language used in school. With everyday reminders, we usually tell someone (or are told by someone) what to remember: *Your meeting is in 15 minutes; pick up milk and eggs on the way home; the car needs to be inspected.* In contrast, reminding language used in school prompts students to recall the established expectations—for transitioning, for staying focused, for working with a lab partner—and then to take positive action based on those expectations.

> **EXAMPLE:** "What will you do to stay focused during our discussion today?" or "Remember our discussion rules."

Reminding language can be used proactively—*before* introducing something new or challenging.

> **EXAMPLE:** "What do you need to do to be ready for next period?"

And it can be used reactively—*after*, or in response to, students' actions.

> **EXAMPLE:** (to a student who begins a side conversation) "What should you be working on now?"

Our use of reminding language sends students the message that we know they are competent learners and have good intentions, even when their behavior gets a little off task. Reminding language works because it enables students to:

➤ **Take responsibility for themselves**—By refraining from telling students what to do, we help them take responsibility for paying attention when we're teaching expectations, for remembering those expectations, and for knowing how to meet them.

➤ **Pause and think first, and then act**—When we use reminding language to prompt students to remember for themselves, they have to stop and think (or visualize) what to do before they take action. This is an essential life skill.

➤ **Develop autonomy and competence**—Proactive reminding language helps guide students toward success in working independently, which increases their confidence and strengthens their sense of self-control and self-motivation. Reactive reminding language can help students quickly get back on track before off-task behavior turns into misbehavior.

How to Use Reminding Language Effectively

Establish clear expectations and refer to them when giving reminders

Throughout the year, teach, model, and have students practice key behaviors that directly connect to expectations. For example, if an expectation is "Treat everyone with respect," the behaviors might be listening carefully when others speak, waiting one's turn to ask a question, and including others.

Once taught, we can refer (either directly or indirectly) to the expectations when giving reminders. This helps students internalize and take responsibility for meeting them. It also clarifies that the purpose of positive behavior is not to please adults, get a reward, or avoid punishment, but to take care of their own learning and that of their classmates.

SITUATION	REMINDING LANGUAGE
The class is transitioning to a new task or activity.	"What should everyone be doing to make our transition as smooth as possible?"

SITUATION	REMINDING LANGUAGE
Students are about to start small-group discussions on an article they read.	*(pointing to an anchor chart)* "Think about the expectations for thoughtful discussions in your groups. How can you meet those expectations today?"

NOTES / REFLECTIONS

Phrase reminders as a question or a statement—and keep them brief

Either a question or a statement works fine for reminding language, as long as we keep it brief. As with all forms of teacher language, the fewer words we use, the better. This gives students the time and space to focus on our central message, think for themselves, and then respond appropriately.

SITUATION	REMINDING LANGUAGE
A student is struggling to do her assignment.	*(privately)* "Jacqui, double-check your assignment sheet. What should you be doing for this part?"

SITUATION	REMINDING LANGUAGE
One group of students keeps interrupting each other during their discussion.	"Show me how you can communicate so everyone has equal talk time."

NOTES / REFLECTIONS

Reminding Language Sentence Starters

➤ Think about _____.

➤ Show us how _____.

➤ Remind everyone how _____.

➤ What if you/we _____?

➤ What might help you _____?

➤ How can you _____?

➤ How do you _____?

➤ Who can tell us _____?

Use proactive and reactive reminders— and keep words and tone neutral

Proactive reminders help students mentally rehearse the appropriate steps to take before they begin a task or activity. Try to think ahead about what might be challenging for students so you can give a proactive reminder to support them.

Reactive reminders support students in correcting themselves when they're just starting to veer off task.

A neutral tone conveys the belief that students can remember expectations and take action to meet them on their own. If our words or tone convey exasperation or doubt, reminders may feel disrespectful or manipulative to students.

SITUATION	REMINDING LANGUAGE
Students are about to conduct their first science experiment with their lab partners.	(*proactively*) "What can you do to help yourselves work effectively together as lab partners?"

SITUATION	REMINDING LANGUAGE
Two students are starting to talk about last night's basketball game rather than working on their assignment.	(*reactively*) "Maria and Sarah, show me what you need to do to complete step one."

NOTES / REFLECTIONS

Use reminders when both you and the student are calm

When we're calm, we're more likely to use neutral words and body language and to convey our trust in students. When students are calm, they're more likely to remember what to do (and then actually do it).

That's why it's important to use reminders before students do something new or something they've struggled with in the past and when their behavior is just starting to go off task.

SITUATION	REMINDING LANGUAGE
Nikki is arguing with her partner and her voice is getting louder.	Try giving Nikki a reminder as soon as you notice her getting upset, saying privately, "Nikki, what can you do to regain self-control so you can talk in a respectful way to Mason?"

SITUATION	REMINDING LANGUAGE
Daniel and John are beginning to arm wrestle rather than work on their project.	Give a reminder as soon as you see them start to arm wrestle. Say privately, "Daniel and John, what are you supposed to be doing right now?"

NOTES / REFLECTIONS

When You Might Use Reminding Language

In this situation	Instead of	Try
When students are working individually	"If you had listened to my directions, you'd know what to do now!" ✳ *Has a sarcastic tone and doesn't prompt students to remember for themselves.*	"What can you do if you're not sure of the directions?" ✳ *Uses a direct, matter-of-fact tone and prompts students to do the remembering.*
Before small-group learning	"You're supposed to complete the checklist first." ✳ *Tells students what to do instead of helping them take responsibility and remember on their own.*	"Before you start the experiment, what do you need to do first?" ✳ *Connects to expectations and prompts students to do the remembering.*
During small-group learning	"You're not listening to each other! You're being rude." ✳ *Has an angry tone and does not express the belief that students can act positively and meet expectations.*	"How can you disagree honestly yet respectfully?" ✳ *Uses a matter-of-fact tone and encourages students to remember how they can meet expectations.*
Before transitions	"You're going to need a pen, your notebook, and your textbook for this assignment." ✳ *Doesn't give students the chance to take responsibility for being prepared.*	"Think about what you'll need for the next assignment. Then take out all materials." ✳ *Focuses students on remembering for themselves how to prepare for the next assignment.*

Tips for Strengthening Reminding Language

Keep reminders respectful, honest, and helpful

When our words, tone, and body language convey openness and trust, students are more likely to feel that we care, to believe they can meet expectations, and to take responsibility for their actions.

> **EXAMPLE:** "You're about to talk about a controversial article on immigration. What can you do to make sure everyone's ideas are heard during the discussion?"

Give reminders before a challenging task

For areas where students have had difficulty in the past and might need extra support, reminding language can help them remember what steps to take to complete the task successfully.

> **EXAMPLE:** If students struggle with transitions, we might say, "Before you move into your small groups, how will you make sure your group is able to get started right away?"

Respond early to signs of off-task behavior

It's important to pay attention to the little things that can lead to bigger behavior challenges—the teasing that results in threats; the bump that leads to a fight. Even minor off-task behavior can quickly escalate, so when we notice small misbehaviors (whether intentional or not), a reminder can get students back on task quickly.

EXAMPLE: If a student says to a classmate, "That's a dumb idea!" right away we might say, "Respectful words only, Lisa."

Follow through

Once we've given a reminder, it's important that we watch or check back to make sure students have acted appropriately. If we don't require follow-through, our reminders lose value over time and students may stop responding to them.

When students do respond to a reminder, a wordless acknowledgment is all that's needed (brief eye contact, smile, nod). If a student continues with off-task behaviors, we can follow through with a redirection (see Chapter 5).

When a Student Needs Repeated Reminders

If a student needs frequent reminders about the same behavior(s), step back and observe—looking for patterns and possible causes—before exploring a solution.

➤ Does a student routinely go off task when working with certain classmates? (Possible solution: Assign the student to different groups.)

➤ Does a student consistently misbehave during specific academic content? (Possible solution: Check that the work is appropriately challenging.)

➤ Does a student seem very sensitive to distractions? (Possible solution: Adjust the routine or procedure, such as by allowing the student to work in a quiet corner rather than at a group table.)

Sometimes, you might decide to talk directly with a student to find out what patterns they notice in their own behavior. Once you have some insight into why the student is having difficulty, you can work together to find a solution.

Reminding Language Practice Chart

Jot down ideas for reminding language you might use with the scenarios given below or adapt language used in the examples on the previous pages. There is also space for you to write your own scenarios and reminding language you might use with them.

SCENARIO	REMINDING LANGUAGE
Students are about to engage in an interactive learning structure or activity that involves working with several different partners.	
Students have just one more class period to work independently and complete their outline for a research paper.	
Two students start chatting during a quiet work time.	
Your scenario:	
Your scenario:	

Reminding Language Self-Reflection Chart

For a week, keep the following chart handy to track how often you use reminding language (use check marks or tally marks). At the end of each day and then for the week, rate yourself to see your growth. Don't worry about keeping an exact count, and stay positive—improving teacher language takes time. With each day you try it, you'll see the results it brings and begin to feel more and more comfortable using it.

	Number of times I used reminding language	Opportunities I missed when I could have used reminding language	Rating my effective use of reminding language 1 = emerging 3 = developing 5 = achieving
Monday			
Tuesday			
Wednesday			
Thursday			
Friday			
Totals			
Notes			

5

Redirecting Language
Getting Students Back On Task

"Hands down. Hold questions until I finish giving all the directions."

"Jason, put away your supplies."

"Try that again using a calm voice and more thoughtful words."

What Is Redirecting Language?

Redirecting language gives students clear, nonnegotiable instructions that direct them to change their behavior to keep everyone safe and on task. Delivered in a tone that's respectful and matter-of-fact, redirecting language helps students regain self-control when they are unable to do so on their own.

EXAMPLE: "Everyone stop. Walk safely to your desks."

The Power of Redirecting Language

Redirecting language enables us to provide the external control students need when their self-control is failing them. Our goal in these situations is to stop the off-task or unsafe behavior right away and then tell students exactly what to do so they can get back to their learning.

> **EXAMPLE:** "Taryn, scissors down. Work on the next part of the assignment."

Ideally, we want to use reinforcing language to promote positive behavior (Chapter 3) and reminding language to prompt students to remember for themselves how to behave (Chapter 4) more frequently than we use redirecting language. But as we all know, students sometimes are too caught up in their off-task behavior to self-correct. Those are the times when they benefit from our clear, firm redirection.

Redirecting language enables students to:

➤ **Stop off-task behavior and return to safe, productive behavior quickly**—A redirection stops the behavior and literally changes a student's direction, mentally and physically.

> **EXAMPLE:** When we say, "Sam, turn around. Wait to hear the directions," a student who's chatting with someone behind them stops and then listens. If two students are arguing over which video game is better, we say, "Stop. Get back to work on your assignments."

➤ **Preserve their dignity and sense of belonging**—With its brevity, clarity, and matter-of-fact tone, redirecting language shows students that they're still respected members of the group. As a result, they're much more likely to accept the redirection and return to positive behavior.

➤ **Know exactly what they need to do**—Misbehaving students have temporarily forgotten the expectations we've taught, so they need explicit instructions that reestablish the expectations by telling them what they need to do *right now*.

> **EXAMPLE:** If Tara is starting her homework when she's supposed to be helping her partner clean up, we might say, "Tara, put that aside. Help Theo clean up the work area."

Skillfully used, redirecting language lets us use our wise external controls to keep students safe and productive while maintaining our positive relationship with them.

How to Use Redirecting Language Effectively

Be direct and specific

When one student is off-task, a public, indirect communication to the whole class—"Someone needs to be more careful with the beaker"—may confuse, embarrass, or cause resentment in the student to whom the comment is really directed. Instead, stand near the student and quietly say, "Carson, put the beaker down."

It's also important to be specific, telling the student exactly what to do. In the moment, students won't necessarily connect an abstract concept ("Get control of yourself") to the concrete behaviors we expect ("Hands down, feet on the floor"); we need to name the desired behavior.

SITUATION	REDIRECTING LANGUAGE
A student is distracting others in her small group.	*(directly and quietly)* "Nadia, come sit over here *(pointing to an empty table)* and work independently."

SITUATION	REDIRECTING LANGUAGE
In health class, there's a discussion on puberty, and some students are getting silly due to the topic.	"All voices off. Then we'll continue."

NOTES / REFLECTIONS

Name only the desired behavior

Redirections work best when you name only the expected behavior ("It's time to listen") rather than the unwanted behavior ("There's too much talking").

The key is to stop and think before giving the redirection: *What do I want the student(s) to do?*

SITUATION	REDIRECTING LANGUAGE
Pairs of students are practicing summarizing what a speaker said, except for one pair, who are trading their own opinions with great excitement.	*(privately to the pair of students)* "Dani, Tenzin, just restate in your own words what the speaker said."

SITUATION	REDIRECTING LANGUAGE
Students have finished cleaning up and some are working on their next assignment, but others have created a circle around a classmate who's performing yo-yo tricks.	"Everyone take your seats now. Start your next assignment."

NOTES / REFLECTIONS

Use brief statements, not questions or suggestions

Redirecting students requires clear, nonnegotiable language. Giving only one, or at most two, concise, action-oriented instructions makes our language easier for students to take in.

If we frame what we want students to do as a question or a suggestion, they may decide to continue with the off-task behavior because we implied they had a choice. Some students might even say "No" and engage us in a power struggle. In off-task moments, students need direct and specific instructions.

SITUATION	REDIRECTING LANGUAGE
A student is providing too much detail and continuing to talk for too long during a whole-group discussion.	"Stop there, Katie, so you have time for people's questions."

SITUATION	REDIRECTING LANGUAGE
Students are excited as they work in pairs exploring a new app on tablets, but the noise level keeps rising.	Signal for quiet attention and say, "Everyone stop. Work quietly on your own."

NOTES / REFLECTIONS

Redirecting Language Sentence Starters

➤ Stop. Put away the _____.

➤ Pause. Get started on _____.

➤ Stop and think. Then raise your hand if _____.

➤ It's time to _____.

➤ Help _____ do _____.

➤ Clean up the _____.

➤ Sit at another desk where you can _____.

➤ Focus on _____.

➤ Right now you need to _____.

Observe and follow through
after giving a redirection

Just as with reminding language (Chapter 4), when we give a redirection we need to make sure students follow it. To do this, we can observe students to check that they get back on task, or we can give a clearer redirection if needed.

When a student does not respond to our redirection, we should follow up with a logical consequence (see box below).

SITUATION	REDIRECTING LANGUAGE
One student is dominating a small group discussion by asserting the same opinion over and over again.	*(moving next to the student and saying quietly)* "Inez, listen to what your group has to say before you speak again" *(standing nearby to monitor the discussion for a few minutes).*

SITUATION	REDIRECTING LANGUAGE
A student keeps jiggling his key ring during independent reading.	*(privately)* "Joe, put your keys in your backpack" *(watching until Joe does this).*

Using a Logical Consequence

When a student doesn't respond to our redirection, we may decide to step in with a logical consequence, such as having the student take a break (Space and Time) to calm down or temporarily lose the privilege of working with a classmate.

For example, if you give the redirection "Use your compass for measuring" and the student continues twirling it around, you might say: "Take some Space and Time. I'll check in with you in a minute."

It's important to avoid naming a consequence when you give a redirection ("Use your compass for measuring or else I'll take it away"). Doing so conveys a negative message—that we doubt students will do the right thing without our stating a consequence. And because these "if you don't _____, I'll _____" statements may feel controlling or threatening to students, they can lead to power struggles.

When we follow through on a redirection that's ignored with an immediate logical consequence, we send a clear message that we mean what we say and the limits we set are nonnegotiable.

When You Might Use Redirecting Language

In this situation	Instead of	Try
When students are working individually	"Would you clean up this mess?" ✳ *Asks a question, which can confuse students or lead to a power struggle.*	(privately) "Lorraine, clean up the supplies." ✳ *Brief redirection given privately sends a clear, respectful message.*
During active teaching	"I suggest that everyone quiet down and stop their side conversations." ✳ *Makes a suggestion, which can confuse students or lead to a power struggle.*	"Stop. Eyes on me. Listen." ✳ *Gives students a clear, brief message about what they need to do.*
During small-group learning	"It looks like someone needs to work harder." ✳ *Sends an indirect message and does not tell the student what action to take.*	(privately) "Ted, finish Part A of your assignment now." ✳ *Addresses the student directly and tells him exactly what to do.*
During whole-group discussions	"I think Sara's got something very interesting to say, so I'd like you to pay attention." ✳ *Implies that pleasing the teacher is what's important and doesn't specify the desired behavior.*	"Pencils down. All eyes on the speaker." ✳ *Focuses on students' actions and is specific in naming the desired behavior.*

Tips for Strengthening Redirecting Language

Teach classroom expectations and review as needed

When we've taught expectations (and reviewed them from time to time), students are more likely to respond appropriately to a redirection. Knowing expectations helps students view a redirection in the context of a positive learning community.

> **EXAMPLE:** When students know the expectation is that everyone helps pick up, we can simply say, "Marcus, back to your work area and help Maria clean up."

If we find ourselves giving frequent redirections, such as during independent work times or transitions, that's a sign for us to stop the class, let everyone settle down, and review or reteach expectations (using reinforcing and reminding language). We risk students tuning us out and ignoring our redirections if we give too many or constantly repeat the same ones.

Get students' attention first

Basic redirecting language, such as "Stop," "Freeze," or "Pause," can put an end to off-task behavior. A nonverbal signal, such as ringing a chime, can also work well. Whether you use a verbal or nonverbal signal, or both, teach students what each signal means and what they should do in response, such as to stop talking and look at you. Then, once students are quiet and focused, they're ready to hear the redirection or next instruction.

Keep your composure

Using a calm, even tone of voice preserves students' dignity by conveying to them that we respect them even when they're not meeting expectations. No matter how frustrated, angry, or disappointed we might be, we want to prevent these emotions from leaking into our communications with students, particularly those who are off task.

> **EXAMPLE:** Eli ignores the reminder you give him and continues to playfully poke Justin in the arm. You can keep your cool by taking a deep breath before saying, "Eli, pause." You can then take another breath before continuing, "Hands to yourself; finish your work sheet."

By taking just a few seconds before speaking, we give ourselves time to collect our thoughts, think of an effective redirection, and deliver it respectfully. If Eli is fully invested in poking Justin despite our redirection, remaining calm will also help us deliver a suitable logical consequence (see page 54), such as having Eli move to a separate work space.

Avoid "Please" and "Thank You"

It's generally appropriate to say "please" when we're asking for a favor and "thank you" in response. However, giving a redirection is not one of those times: we're not asking students to do us a favor, we're telling them how to meet an agreed-upon expectation.

Similarly, avoid "I like how you . . ." or "I need you to . . ." wording; this suggests that students should choose behavior to please us, rather than to be responsible members of a classroom community.

Redirecting Language Practice Chart

Jot down ideas for redirecting language you might use with the scenarios given below or adapt language used in the examples on the previous pages. There is also space for you to write your own scenarios and redirecting language you might use with them.

SCENARIO	REDIRECTING LANGUAGE
As students wait in line to leave your room, one student hooks his leg around his friend's and says, "Can you beat the wrestling champion of the world?"	
For the third time during a class discussion, a student leans over and whispers to her neighbor.	
During a small-group activity to review vocabulary words, you notice one group making up nonsense definitions.	
Your scenario:	
Your scenario:	

Redirecting Language Self-Reflection Chart

For a week, keep the following chart handy to track how often you use redirecting language (use check marks or tally marks). At the end of each day and then for the week, rate yourself to see your growth. Don't worry about keeping an exact count, and stay positive—improving teacher language takes time. With each day you try it, you'll see the results it brings and begin to feel more and more comfortable using it.

	Number of times I used redirecting language	Opportunities I missed when I could have used redirecting language	Rating my effective use of redirecting language 1 = emerging 3 = developing 5 = achieving
Monday			
Tuesday			
Wednesday			
Thursday			
Friday			
Totals			
Notes			

6

Open-Ended Questions
Stretching Students' Academic and Social Learning

"What evidence in the text do you think best supports the author's claims? What makes you think so?"

"How did you and your partner reach that solution? What led you both to agree on using that particular strategy?"

"If you could do this over, what would you do differently to improve your group's performance?"

What Are Open-Ended Questions?

Open-ended questions are those with no predetermined right or wrong answer; instead, they invite students to respond with any reasoned or relevant thoughts. By drawing on students' own ideas, knowledge, skills, experiences, and feelings, these questions stretch their curiosity, reasoning ability, creativity, and independence. As a result, students learn more broadly and deeply. Open-ended questions can also give us a snapshot of what students know (and the thinking that led to that knowledge) as well as any misconceptions they may have.

The Power of Open-Ended Questions

Open-ended questions spark students' engagement in their learning by encouraging them to think for themselves, analyze information, make connections among ideas, share knowledge, and connect personally to the content.

> **EXAMPLE:** To introduce a lesson on daily life in countries with limited energy resources, a teacher asks the class, "In the countries we'll examine today, electricity may be available for only a few hours a day. Take a minute to think about all the ways you use electricity. What would you miss if you couldn't have electricity whenever you wanted it?"

As students respond, the teacher builds on their ideas by asking additional open-ended questions, such as "What strategies might people in these countries use to get things done when they don't have electricity? What strategies could we use if we didn't have electricity for a week at school?"

Open-ended questions benefit students by:

➤ **Putting students at the center**—When we use open-ended questions, we typically talk less and students talk more, which promotes their critical thinking skills and lets them see the important role they play in their own learning.

➤ **Supporting the learning cycle**—Students' responses to open-ended questions at the three points in the learning cycle help them develop more sophisticated thinking and knowledge, which leads to even richer learning. First, these questions can support students in generating ideas and goals: "What are some ways you might use a spreadsheet?" Then, they can help students actively explore, experiment, and problem-solve: "How else could you sort and retrieve the data?" Afterward, open-ended questions can lead students to reflect on their experiences: "What did you learn about spreadsheets that surprised you during this exploration?"

The Learning Cycle

Generating ideas and goals

Actively exploring, experimenting, problem-solving

Reflecting on experiences

➤ **Developing thinking skills**—To answer open-ended questions effectively, students need to think deeply. Thus, they're more likely to use higher-order thinking skills—prediction, analysis, synthesis, comparison/contrast, evaluation, and creativity—than when we use closed-ended questions or simply tell them what they need to know.

➤ **Encouraging self-awareness**—Open-ended questions help students become aware of how their choices affect themselves and others.

EXAMPLE: Asking "How did you make sure everyone in your group had an equal chance to share their ideas?" prompts students to reflect on how their choice of actions (such as taking turns speaking) shaped their group's discussion. As students become more aware of how their behavior affects others, they're more likely to choose responsible, productive courses of action.

➤ **Building a sense of community**—Students who have frequent opportunities to answer open-ended questions become more aware of their own thinking, values, and interests, as well as those of others in the class. Hearing diverse points of view enriches and deepens everyone's learning, gives students a chance to know each other better, and enables them to practice empathy. This in turn can help students feel safe and valued, increasing their willingness to support each other and to take positive risks essential for growth.

Using open-ended questions shows trust in students' ability to think for themselves, to come up with reasonable ideas, and to contribute in valuable ways to the class. As a result, students are likely to develop a stronger sense of autonomy, competence, and belonging—feelings that lead to greater engagement and investment in their learning.

How to Use Open-Ended Questions Effectively

Convey your curiosity

If we truly wish to learn what students are thinking, asking open-ended questions—answers to which we are genuinely curious to hear—is a positive way to convey that wish to students.

Our curiosity tells students that their ideas are welcomed and valued and prompts them to trust us more. As a result, they're more willing to take chances in sharing ideas and stretching their thinking.

SITUATION	OPEN-ENDED QUESTION
Students are being introduced to a new unit on probability.	"What do you know about using math to make predictions?"
SITUATION	OPEN-ENDED QUESTION
Students are preparing to do a challenging assignment.	"How can we help each other be successful? If you get stuck, what can you do to keep making progress?"

Open-Ended Questions Starters

➤ What are some ways that _____?

➤ What are some things you _____?

➤ What surprised you about _____?

➤ How might you _____?

➤ How did you support your group today? Describe one way.

➤ How could you say that using your own words?

➤ When would be a good time to _____?

➤ When might you try using _____?

➤ Where else do you see _____?

➤ Why might you choose _____ instead of _____?

Clarify what you're asking for or seeking

Even when we want to hear a broad range of responses, setting some boundaries helps students focus. If we want students to compare two characters, asking "What did you notice about this character?" may or may not elicit character comparisons.

But if we add "I'm looking for your ideas on how this character is similar to and different from the main character in our last story," we've established boundaries for students' responses while still welcoming all relevant and reasonable responses.

SITUATION	OPEN-ENDED QUESTION
Students are using mapping software as part of a unit on ancient world cultures.	"How could you use mapping software to learn about the daily lives of people in this region?"

SITUATION	OPEN-ENDED QUESTION
A student has been struggling whenever asked to work as part of a small group.	(*privately*) "What are some ways you can contribute to your group's work today?" If needed, point out any helpful supports they can use such as an anchor chart.

NOTES / REFLECTIONS

Use words that encourage cooperation, not competition

Avoid open-ended questions that could unintentionally lead to competition or imply that some responses are more acceptable than others, such as "Who has a better idea about . . ." or "What's a better way to say that?" These can lead to some students trying to outdo classmates in coming up with the "best" answer; others might shut down completely.

To facilitate rich discussions, phrase questions so that they prompt students to collaborate with one another, using "another idea" or "some different ideas." And inviting ideas from all students helps create a tone of collaboration.

SITUATION	OPEN-ENDED QUESTION
Students are presenting the results of their surveys by making and displaying a series of graphs.	"If you could revise your graphs, what are some other ideas for how you'd do that?"
SITUATION	OPEN-ENDED QUESTION
A class is discussing ideas for good nutrition and improving eating habits.	"What tips for healthy eating have you read or heard about that people might want to consider? What makes you think so?"
SITUATION	OPEN-ENDED QUESTION
A group has had difficulty working together on a task. Before they begin the next task, you speak with them privately.	"Think about our expectations for working together." Give the students a moment to think about these or to look at an anchor chart of them. Then ask, "How can our expectations help you work together to complete this task? What can each of you do to support your team members?"

NOTES / REFLECTIONS

Use wait time

Pausing for a few seconds before calling on students to respond can lead to more thoughtful answers. Those who are typically quick to respond can benefit from waiting to be called on and hearing other perspectives; those who need more time to think get a chance to formulate a reasoned response.

An additional benefit of pausing is that you're modeling for students the importance of being patient and thoughtful.

SITUATION	OPEN-ENDED QUESTION
Students are learning how to solve a new type of equation.	After asking, "How many different ways can we come up with for solving this equation?" don't ask for ideas right away. Instead, say, "On your own, jot down some ideas." Give students a minute or so to do this before asking them to raise their hands and share ideas.
SITUATION	OPEN-ENDED QUESTION
Some students immediately raise their hands and wave them around whenever a question is asked.	Signal for quiet attention. Once everyone has put their hands down, briefly remind them of the expectation to keep hands down until you're ready to call on students for answers. Then repeat the question and silently count to five before asking for a show of hands.

NOTES / REFLECTIONS

Use open-ended questions at each stage of your lesson

At the start of a new lesson, topic, or unit, open-ended questions can spark students' interest and enable them to make personal connections to what they're about to learn.

Using open-ended questions throughout a lesson increases students' knowledge of the content by enabling them to think more deeply and hear other perspectives.

As you close a lesson, open-ended questions prompt students to reflect on their learning, the process or thinking they used, and their effort.

SITUATION	OPEN-ENDED QUESTION
As you introduce a lesson on mass, you show students a photo of various types of containers.	"What do you notice about these containers? Which do you think is the heaviest? Why?"
SITUATION	OPEN-ENDED QUESTION
Students are working in small groups trying to plan the next step in building a robot. One group seems to be stuck.	"Where are you stuck? How can I help?"
SITUATION	OPEN-ENDED QUESTION
Students are wrapping up the projects they've worked on in small groups.	"What's one contribution you made to your group that you're proud of? What collaborative efforts did you make as a group today? How did those help you finish up your project?"

NOTES / REFLECTIONS

When You Might Use
Open-Ended Questions

In this situation	Instead of	Try
During active teaching	"Whose point of view does the introduction to this article show?" ✳ *Closed-ended question that simply asks students to recall information.*	"What about the introduction to this article helps you predict the author's argument?" ✳ *Guides students to focus on a higher-level thinking skill—in this case, how to analyze an effective introduction for a persuasive essay. Puts boundaries around the question while keeping it open-ended.*
Before small-group learning	"Who has a better idea for making sure all group members are heard?" ✳ *Encourages competition among students.*	"What are some different ideas for making sure all group members are heard?" ✳ *Encourages cooperation.*
After whole-group discussions	"Wow! We spent 20 minutes on that discussion and shared a lot of great ideas. Let's go quickly around the room; which one do you think we should focus on first?" Immediately calls on the first student who raised a hand. ✳ *Doesn't give any wait time, so many students won't have a chance to formulate thoughtful answers.*	"What's one thing you heard in this discussion that you're still curious about? Take 15 seconds to think …" Pause 15 seconds before taking student responses. ✳ *Gives wait time. Encourages students to think before speaking; allows students who need more time to formulate answers an equal chance of being heard.*

In this situation	Instead of	Try
While students are working on their own	"Is this appropriate to cite as evidence?" hoping the student will reply, "No, I guess it doesn't really make sense." <p align="center">✳</p> *Sounds like an open-ended question, but hidden in it is the teacher's desire to hear a certain answer. Students can often detect such pseudo open-ended questions and may shut down their thinking as a result.*	"What's your thinking behind citing that as evidence?" asked with genuine curiosity. <p align="center">✳</p> *Effective open-ended questions are ones asked with true curiosity. If a student made a mistake that you need to point out, try making a statement. For example, "Remember that in this case, your evidence needs to be a fact."*
In one-on-one conversations with you	"How do you feel about your lab work?" <p align="center">✳</p> *Students may not know what the teacher means by "feel" or which aspect of their lab work to think about. They're likely to answer—honestly— "I don't know."*	"What are some things you think you did well in this week's experiment?" <p align="center">✳</p> *Refers to concrete experiences. Students can think back to actual actions they did in this week's experiment. If your goal is to have students think about their lab work in general, guide them toward that after asking them about a few concrete experiences.*

Tips for Strengthening Open-Ended Questions

Use words such as *might*, *may*, *could*, or *possibly*

"What *might* you do to gather information for your research project?" Words such as these signal to students that they're free to brainstorm because you're just looking for possible ideas. In contrast, "What *will* you do to gather information for your research project?" suggests that you're looking for one specific answer or a commitment to a course of action.

Use words such as *some people* and *some students*

When students feel that their answers are hypothetical (and don't have to reflect their own personal views or experiences), they're more likely to share ideas. This technique is especially helpful when discussing sensitive topics such as behavior issues or academic areas that a student struggles with.

> **EXAMPLE:** Asking "Why might *some* students find it difficult to organize information in their writing?" rather than "Why do *you* find it difficult to organize information in your writing?" takes the pressure off students and allows them to expand their thinking so they can consider more solutions.

There's a Place for Closed-Ended Questions

Closed-ended questions have a definite place in our teaching. In fact, it would be hard to teach without them. This type of question is essential when you want to check students' understanding of a fact ("How many electrons does a hydrogen atom have?") or get specific information from them ("Who is presenting for your group?").

That said, your teaching will be more powerful if most of your questions to students are open-ended ones that invite them to wonder, think, and share their ideas.

Specifically encourage multiple perspectives

Using words such as *how many*, *different*, and *other* in your open-ended questions tells students that you want to hear a variety of answers. You can also follow your question with a challenge.

> **EXAMPLE:** "What are some different ways you might show your results? Let's see how many ideas we can list."

Choose words that cue students' thinking processes

Students often have an easier time responding to open-ended questions when you name the thinking process they'll need to use to answer them. One way to do this is to embed a cue word in the question, such as *brainstorm*, *predict*, *evaluate*, *compare and contrast*, or *persuade*.

> **EXAMPLE:** "What might the antagonist choose to do next? Make some *predictions* based on what you've read so far." This strategy works best when you've already taught students what the named thinking process means and given them a chance to practice it.

Make sure your open-ended questions are truly open-ended

A question is open-ended only when you really want to hear what students think. Even a question that begins with "What do you think . . . ?" can be closed-ended if you have a specific answer in mind. Frequently asking questions that sound open-ended when you're actually seeking a specific answer can confuse students and dampen their efforts at critical thinking. Some students may start to guess at the answer you want; others may simply wait until you state the correct answer.

An easy test for open-endedness: Ask yourself if you have a specific answer in mind. If so, ask a closed-ended question or make a statement.

Aim for the specific and concrete

A question that's too broad or abstract can be harder for students to answer. Keep your open-ended questions specific, and remember to give students some boundaries.

> **EXAMPLE:** Rather than asking, "How are you going to approach your essay?" try "Which of the strategies we've studied do you think will work best to get your point across in this essay? What's your thinking behind that choice?"

Respond directly and calmly to sarcastic or jokey answers

If students answer by making a joke or being sarcastic, respond directly to their words and then calmly steer their attention back to the question. Suppose you ask the class, "Why do you think this set of problems felt harder than usual?" and a student answers, "Because we're all bad at math!" You might respond, "Sometimes when we struggle with something, we feel we're bad at it. But everyone in here can learn—you've proven it all year. So let's take another look at the problems. What about them seems difficult or confusing?"

Open-Ended Questions Practice Chart

Jot down ideas for open-ended questions you might use with the scenarios given below or adapt language used in the examples on the previous pages. There is also space for you to write your own scenarios and open-ended questions you might use with them.

SCENARIO	OPEN-ENDED QUESTION
Students are about to read the next chapter or section of a textbook.	
Students are listening as you teach a new concept.	
Students are reflecting on their efforts in completing a challenging assignment.	
Your scenario:	
Your scenario:	

Open-Ended Questions Self-Reflection Chart

For a week or so, keep the following chart handy to track how often you use open-ended questions (use check marks or tally marks). At the end of each day and then for the week, rate yourself to see your growth. Don't worry about keeping an exact count, and stay positive—improving teacher language takes time. With each day you practice using open-ended questions, you'll see the results they bring and feel more comfortable using them.

	Number of times I used open-ended questions	Opportunities I missed when I could have used open-ended questions	Rating my effective use of open-ended questions 1 = emerging 3 = developing 5 = achieving
Monday			
Tuesday			
Wednesday			
Thursday			
Friday			
Totals			
Notes			

Teacher Language Summary Chart

	Purpose	Example	Key Tip
Envisioning	Paints a clear and enticing picture that helps students see themselves behaving and achieving in ways that connect to, but go beyond, what they already know and can do.	"Your projects show that you have a strong understanding of the rock cycle. Just as geologists do, you'll be able to use that understanding to make sense of some of the unusual formations we'll see on our field trip."	Because students will want to live up to the vision when they sense that you truly believe they can, be sure to name only skills, capabilities, and behaviors you're convinced are within their reach.
Reinforcing	Helps students build on their strengths by naming what they're doing well.	"You listened carefully to each other and asked thoughtful questions. That helped bring out a lot of really interesting ideas during this discussion."	By naming concrete and specific positive actions, students know what's working well and that the steps they're taking are going in the right direction.
Reminding	Prompts students to remember expectations (or rules). Helps students correct themselves when their behavior is just beginning to go off task.	"It's been awhile since we've used the temperature sensors. What do you remember about handling them safely?" To students just beginning a side conversation during a class discussion: "Clayton, Mariah—discussion rules."	Students can remember only what they've already learned, so be sure you've taught the action or behavior before giving a reminder about it.
Redirecting	Gives students clear, nonnegotiable instructions to correct behavior that is clearly off task (versus just beginning to go off task).	To a group of students talking about the latest movie when they're supposed to be having a small-group discussion: "End this conversation. Get back to the discussion topic on your assignment sheet."	To protect middle schoolers' dignity and preserve your positive relationship with them, keep your words and tone firm but respectful.
Open-Ended Questions	Help students learn more broadly and deeply by drawing on their knowledge, skills, experiences, and feelings as a way to stretch their curiosity, reasoning ability, creativity, and independence.	"What parallels do you see between kings in Shakespeare's time and current-day politicians?"	You can tell if your question is truly open-ended by asking yourself, "Do I have a specific answer in mind?" If the answer is "No, I'm open to any reasoned and relevant response," then your question is open-ended.

About the Publisher

Center for Responsive Schools, Inc., a not-for-profit educational organization, is the developer of *Responsive Classroom*®, a research-based education approach associated with greater teacher effectiveness, higher student achievement, and improved school climate. *Responsive Classroom* practices help educators build competencies in four interrelated domains: engaging academics, positive community, effective management, and developmentally responsive teaching. We offer the following resources for educators:

PROFESSIONAL DEVELOPMENT SERVICES

➤ Workshops for K–8 educators (locations around the country and internationally)

➤ On-site consulting services to support implementation

➤ Resources for site-based study

➤ Annual conferences for K–8 educators

PUBLICATIONS AND RESOURCES

➤ Books on a wide variety of *Responsive Classroom* topics

➤ Professional development kits for school-based study

➤ Free monthly newsletter

➤ Extensive library of free articles on our website

FOR DETAILS, CONTACT:

Responsive Classroom®

Center for Responsive Schools, Inc.
85 Avenue A, P.O. Box 718
Turners Falls, Massachusetts 01376-0718

800-360-6332   www.responsiveclassroom.org
info@responsiveclassroom.org